# CLOUDS

## WEATHER REPORT

Ann and Jim Merk

The Rourke Corporation, Inc.
Vero Beach, Florida 32964

PHOTO CREDITS
© Jerry Hennen: cover; courtesy NASA: page 8; © Lynn M. Stone:
all other photos

**Library of Congress Cataloging-in-Publication Data**

Merk, Ann, 1952–
    Clouds / by Ann and Jim Merk
        p. cm. — (Weather report)
    Includes index
    ISBN 0-86593-389-8
    1. Clouds—Juvenile literature.  2. Weather—Juvenile literature.
[1. Clouds.]
I. Merk, Jim, 1952- .  II. Title   III. Series: Merk, Ann, 1952-  Weather
report.
QC921.35.M47  1994
551.57'6—dc20                               94-13324
                                                CIP
Printed in the USA                              AC

# TABLE OF CONTENTS

# CLOUDS

Clouds are like fingerprints in the sky—no two are alike. Some look like puffs of whipped cream. Some rear upwards like great, grey wild horses. Others are drawn across the sky like white threads.

Scientists place clouds into several groups. Being able to tell one kind of cloud from another helps scientists and other people to **forecast**, or predict, the weather.

*A kite climbs toward "zebra stripes" in the sky*

## HOW CLOUDS FORM

Even when rain isn't falling, the air contains **moisture**, or water. Water that we cannot see in the air is called **water vapor**.

Clouds develop when a mass of cool air strikes warm, wet air. Clouds form because billions of tiny particles of water **condense**, or join together. They form droplets attached to specks of dust.

*Clouds form when*
*water particles condense*

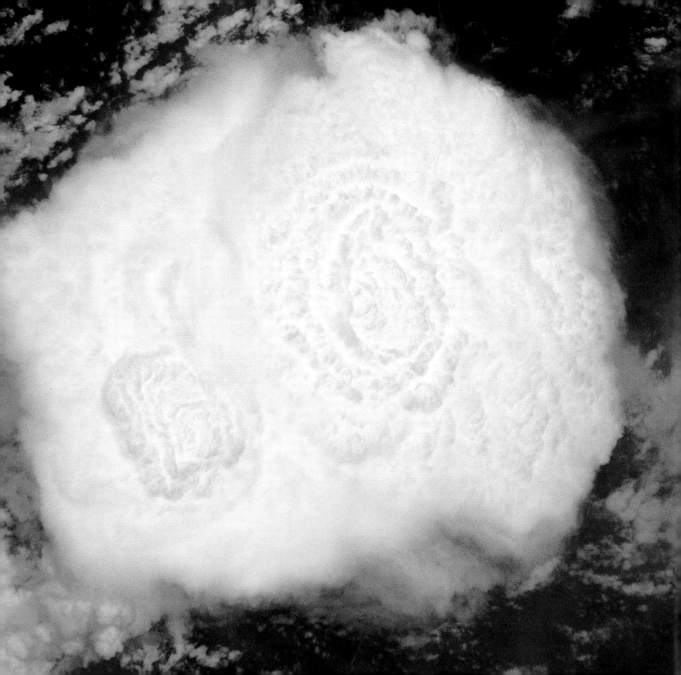

# CLOUDS OF MANY KINDS

Clouds are certainly different in looks. They are also different in where they are and what they do.

Scientists group clouds according to their shape, their moisture level and their **altitude**, or height, above the ground. Three broad groups of clouds are **cirrus**, **cumulus** and **stratus**. Many cloud formations are a mixture of types.

*This huge thirty-mile wide thunderstorm over Niger was photographed by American astronauts who were 150 miles above it*

# THREE KINDS OF CLOUDS

Stratus clouds spread like grey sheets across the sky. They can be thick or thin, and they can be high or low in the sky.

Cumulus clouds are puffy. They are usually low. Sometimes, though, they stack up like pillows upon each other and climb 35,000 feet or more. That height, about seven miles above the Earth, is where many jet airliners fly.

Cirrus clouds are usually the highest clouds. They are thin, feathery clouds made of tiny ice drops instead of water.

*Cumulus clouds drift over a Florida salt marsh*

Passengers flying 35,000 feet high in a jet look down on a white world of clouds

*High cirrus clouds wander over New Hampshire's Presidential Range peaks*

## RAIN CLOUDS

Puffy white cumulus clouds usually mean fair weather. But certain kinds of cumulus clouds can produce rain.

The tall, puffy pillars in the sky we call "thunderheads" are a type of cumulus cloud. Thunderheads deliver thunder, lightning and hard rains.

Stratus clouds can also bring rain. Cirrus clouds are not rain clouds, but they often signal a change from fair to foul weather.

*Moisture-filled rain clouds hang over the Aleutian Islands of Alaska*

# FOG AND SMOG

You don't have to be a giant to have your head in the clouds. Each time you step outside into fog your head is in a stratus cloud. Fog is simply a stratus cloud at ground level.

Fog forms when the ground is warm and the air is cool and moist.

**Smog** is a mixture of smoke, air pollution and fog. Cities like Los Angeles and Mexico City have an especially hard time with smog.

*A Florida fisherman races his boat through morning fog*

# THE COLOR OF CLOUDS

Some clouds are white because the tiny droplets of water or ice in them act like mirrors. In reflecting the light of the sun, they look white.

Thick clouds look dark because little sunlight can pass through them.

Sooner or later clouds lose their color and their moisture. When the cloud's moisture is used up, the cloud vanishes.

*In the light of a setting sun, clouds*
*take on bright colors*

# THE CLOUDS AND SUN

On cloudy days the sun seems to disappear. The sun is still shining, but we can't see the sun because clouds block our view. Clouds are to the sun what a shade is to a light bulb.

Clouds don't block all the sun's light. Even on cloudy days, some of the sun's light reaches Earth and we still enjoy a period of daylight.

*Even under a grey blanket of stratus clouds, a cougar has plenty of light in which to hunt*

# ABOVE THE CLOUDS

Above the layers of clouds, the sun shines brightly. People riding in jet airplanes may leave the airport on a cloudy day. But within minutes their flight carries them upward through the clouds. The airplane flies in sunlight.

Passenger planes fly six and seven miles above the ground. Clouds rarely form much higher than that, so passengers enjoy a clear view above, if not below.

## Glossary

**altitude** (AL tuh tood) — the height of something above ground

**cirrus** (SEER us) — thin and wispy white clouds made up of tiny ice particles at high altitudes

**condense** (KUN dents) — to bring together

**cumulus** (QUM yuh lus) — puffy clouds that sometimes pile into tall thunderheads

**forecast** (FOR kast) — to predict, especially to predict the weather

**moisture** (MOIST ur) — wetness

**smog** (SMAHG) — a haze created by a mixture of smoke, air pollution and fog

**stratus** (STRAH tuss) — a wide, covering cloud usually at 2,000 to 7,000 feet above the ground

**water vapor** (WAW ter VAY pur) — water that is part of the air; water in its gaseous state

# INDEX